THE UNIQUE CLASSROOM

Transforming Lives Through Unique Teaching Methods

"Awarded 40 Under 40 Top Accounting Professional in the US - CPA Practice advisor, USA."

SRIPAL JAIN CA, CPA USA

INDIA • SINGAPORE • MALAYSIA

ISBN

Hardcase 979-8-89519-505-5
Paperback 979-8-89498-352-3

For more information, email sripaljain07@gmail.com.

CONTENTS

ACKNOWLEDGEMENT

This journey wouldn't have been possible without the unwavering support of my family, friends, and most importantly, my students. To the thirteen featured voices and the countless others who have entrusted us with their aspirations, thank you for sharing your stories and inspiring others. Your success is the true mark of achievement for our institute.

Finally, a heartfelt thanks to you, the reader. Your dedication to learning fuels my passion to teach. May this book empower you to achieve your goals.

Conventional teaching methods and rigid educational systems often stifle the power and potential of learning. Learning should not only transform our understanding but also broaden our perspectives. Simandhar Education firmly believes that every individual is unique and, with the right support, guidance, and inspiration, students can achieve great heights in their chosen field. It is a space where dreams are not only nurtured but also realized. In the distinctive classrooms of Simandhar Education, paths are forged, and destinies are shaped.

Through thirteen compelling stories of resilience, determination, and triumph, it becomes evident that Simandhar Education offers students and aspirants a beacon of hope in a world of fierce competition and demanding standards.

Chapter 01

BEYOND THE CLASSROOM

While succinctly capturing my multifaceted role as a coach, mentor, and entrepreneur in a few words might be challenging, I can say that my core purpose lies in empowering individuals. I achieve this through Simandhar Education, a leading educational institute for international CPA, CMA, EA courses. Here, me and my team equip aspiring accounting and finance professionals, particularly those seeking the CPA, CMA or EA designation, with the knowledge and skills to excel in their chosen fields. Witnessing our students achieve their dreams and scale new heights of success is a constant source of motivation and reinforces my passion for leading Simandhar Education and guiding its dedicated students.

Simandhar Education transcends a typical coaching-teaching-training institute. It embodies the culmination of lifelong inspirations that have shaped my approach to education. My earliest influences were my mother and sister-in-law, who instilled in me a relentless pursuit of problem-solving. Fuelled by my mother's unwavering dedication – exemplified by her willingness to tackle complex challenges like conquering a difficult algebraic equation during my school years – Simandhar Education is built upon the same core principle. We approach each student's challenges with unwavering dedication, mirroring my mother's enduring support, ensuring no problem goes unresolved.

My interest in teaching wasn't an immediate realization but rather a path revealed by my sister-in-law. Her keen observation of my abilities identified a potential for a fulfilling career in education, which ultimately propelled me in that direction.

Simandhar Education benefited greatly from the mentorship of prominent figures in the business world. Devendra Bagree, Managing Director of Standard Chartered Bank, provided invaluable guidance and insights on operational issues and coaching strategies, shaping the institute's current form through numerous consultations. Similarly, Amit Agarwal, Partner at BDO, one of the world's leading audit firms, played a crucial role in my leadership development at Simandhar Education. Their combined expertise helped me navigate challenges inherent to scaling a business, including effective delegation and workload management.

There are three distinctive aspects to my vision in life. First is to be able to contribute to a student's professional aspiration. The second is to create an environment that fosters and creates confident, capable and talented individuals in the field of finance and accounting and the third is to create a lasting impact on every student I interact with. The foundation of Simandhar lies in this vision of mine which has always been clear right from the beginning. Monetising our premium placement services was something that took time to get right though. We never charge the students, but we believe that our students are all groomed, trained, and mentored with high standards and thus an asset to our organization. This is how the talent pool and portal of Simandhar have been established. Our placements are with top-quality organizations and large conglomerates who are willing to be charged for such exceptional candidates in the roles that are offered.

I also have a very strict policy of not overworking my team or the students. That is why Simandhar Education is one of the few start-ups that have a 5-day work week culture. I deliberately avoided replicating the culture of most organizations where some days work goes on until the wee hours of the morning.

I don't believe in a work-life balance as such. What I do believe and follow through is the ability to prioritize work whenever necessary. Balance is not always feasible nor possible in work and life, but by prioritizing things that need to be done when they need to be done, is more effective and results in a better outcome. Instead of this commonly used term 'work-life balance' I would prefer to use the concept called 'availability'. Being available to de-escalate an issue of high importance or in situations of emergencies is what should really matter – whether at work or in life.

I don't need added motivation in life or work. I genuinely love my job. I love teaching. This makes every day at Simandhar exciting and invigorating. My work revolves less around the commercial aspects and more around the joy I get from teaching, mentoring and encouraging my students. I have a saying: "When you don't do things for money you're automatically motivated. But when you do things for money, you become greedy, never motivated." I believe satisfaction can never come from just making money. True satisfaction comes from passion. It has to come from something greater than money and bigger than oneself, which is passion. Once we cross the boundaries of passion, we become compassionate. Today I see myself as more compassionate than merely passionate. I am innately impacted and affected by the struggles, problems, and challenges students face. Unanswered questions bother me and I find myself trying to answer as many as I can. Helping students in whichever way I can is something that comes very naturally to me. I can neither control it nor camouflage it. It is called compassion and I understand how it can be misused but nevertheless, this is who I am and who I will continue to be. Nothing done in half measures! That is who I intrinsically am in five words.

Simandhar Education began as a response to the increasing number of training requests that I kept getting while initially teaching students part-time at other CA coaching institutes. Correcting national-level CA papers additionally offered me insights into the general way students grasped the subjects, the lacuna in their understanding of important concepts and the crucial aspects of the subject matter. This is when I decided that Simandhar Education would design courses that would serve to bridge the gap between learning and understanding the skills of finance and accounting as well as being able to apply that knowledge in the real-world scenario.

Today I can proudly say that Simandhar Education is one of the finest and most sought out Institute for those aspiring for a CPA, CMA and/ or EA certification and/or other finance/accounting skills. However, the journey of establishing a team, setting up systems, and structuring the training modules was not that easy. The struggles and challenges I faced were daunting and difficult but giving up has never been (and will never be) an option for me. I remember relentlessly knocking on the doors of numerous corporate offices and companies introducing the programs and training modules of Simandhar. The callbacks or the responses would come, if at all, after long waiting periods, that too after countless follow-up calls. Finally, I landed one account with Virtusa. Encouraged by that one positive response, I started aggressively reaching out by mail and other means to increase the number of corporate clients. Through a contact known to me, I secured a prestigious Reliance account in Mumbai. The session was scheduled to be at Jio Auditorium with 170 cameras and a seating capacity of 800 people. A session of this scale eventually catapulted me to various other big accounts such as Barclay's, Amazon, and other Big 4 companies etc. There was no looking back for Simandhar Education after exposure at such a global level.

Keeping my main focus on teaching, mentoring, and counseling students pursuing CPA, I also did a deep dive into every student's NASBA's (National Association of State Boards of Accountancy, USA) eligibility and evaluation process. This is a lengthy, complicated, and strenuous exercise. I would sit the whole night sorting complicated eligibility issues to ensure I secured eligibility to as many students as I possibly could. I even went to the extent of challenging the NASBA report and getting it changed to make more students eligible. That got me recognised and rewarded by none other than the NASBA president who invited me for lunch. This instantly gave me a level of credibility that no other globally recognised financial and accounting body could ever accord me. Recognition from a regulatory body such as NASBA offered me unprecedented acceptance and status as a recommendable and reliable CPA/CMA/EA expert.

As I witness the exponential growth and achievements of Simandhar's students, some of them winning the prestigious Elijah Watts Sell awards, I can't help but feel a sense of personal triumph. I now believe I have the capability to guide students, create CPA world toppers and put Simandhar Education on the CPA/CMA/EA world map. I am so inspired by my faculty at Simandhar Education. They have a very interesting and interactive method of teaching the students and getting them involved in the classroom sessions. Some of the faculty (like Suraj and Akshay) go beyond the regular teaching techniques by adopting the use of excel and other in-depth methods. I see them continuously improving their teaching methods and creating innovative ways to make the sessions more engaging. Surendra is someone who inspires me by her slow teaching method and approach to taking her classes. I generally go on speed mode in my class, but seeing her makes me want to adopt a similar teaching and talking manner too.

The bedrock of my life's purpose is having the privilege to teach, mentor, and interact with various students constantly and consistently through different means. Whether it is in the classrooms, or through WhatsApp groups or through Telegram groups that have around 30,000 students. I make it a point to answer their queries, engage with them, adding value to the courses and constantly keep the CPA/CMA/EA professional momentum going strong.

My message to my students has always been for them to focus on the courses and studies and I will ensure the rest is being taken care of. When a student becomes a part of Simandhar, I feel a great sense of responsibility to instill clarity in subjects, confidence in scoring well in the exams, and achieving the best in the international world of finance and accountancy.

If there is one thing I would like to change in today's times though is to help inculcate the habit of reading and keeping up to date with current affairs in all students. I find that nowadays there is an acute lack of curiosity and interest in reading the newspapers. I don't find students trying to learn something beyond the classrooms or subject textbooks. This is a habit that I want to encourage my students to embrace.

'The Monk Who Sold His Ferrari' by Robin Sharma is my favorite book. Being spiritually inclined, the philosophy espoused in the book resonates with me. I am a follower of the Jain monk, Simandhar Swami, after whom my institute is named. The philosophy of Simandhar Swami focuses on creating a positive impact on the outer world while focusing on our inner well-being too. There is also another philosophy I adhere to which is apologizing whenever I am wrong. I believe the more we apologise, the more consciously aware we become of our mistakes, thus we are then better able to correct and reduce those mistakes and evolve overall as a better being.

I also believe in the tenet 'never hurt a living creature no matter what'. Every living being and all life's forms however big or small is precious and sacred. I ardently practice meditation every day for 45 minutes. This gives me a lot of peace and calm and I am able to focus on work better after it.

How would I like to be remembered? Well, that's simple to answer. As a great teacher, mentor, and entrepreneur.

Chapter 02

HARDER THE STRUGGLE, SWEETER THE FRUIT

Introduction:

A story of resilience and determination, Ankur Yadav's professional journey is nothing short of spectacular. From delivering meals to mastering numbers Ankur scaled the heights of academic success through sheer grit and persistence. Through unwavering dedication and the unstinting support of our unique classroom, Ankur defied the odds and propelled himself toward a future filled with promise and opportunity.

While employed as a delivery executive with Zomato, Ankur concurrently pursued the CMA course through Simandhar Education. Simultaneously, he secured an internship opportunity with Infosys facilitated by Simandhar Education, which eventually led to a full-time position upon completion of the certification. Ankur's outstanding performance at Infosys garnered him the prestigious "Best Debutant" award from Infosys Limited.

Q&A with Ankur:

Q: Can you share your initial experiences as a Zomato delivery boy and how you transitioned into the world of finance?

Since my college days, I've demonstrated a strong aptitude for economics and business management, particularly excelling in finance—an area that has always piqued my genuine interest. Naturally I felt drawn to pursuing a career in this field. However, life presented its challenges. Hailing from a financially disadvantaged background, our situation took a turn for the worse when my father lost his job during the COVID-19 pandemic.

With limited options available and aware of the burgeoning economy in India, I made the decision to take on a demanding role as a Zomato delivery executive. Despite the gruelling schedule, often spanning 14 to 15 hours per day and the meagre daily earnings of 600-700 rupees, I persisted. While my mother fretted over my well-being, I persevered for 7 to 8 months, navigating through delivering meals to Covid patients and enduring harsh monsoon conditions.

These experiences served as a crucible, strengthening my resolve to carve out a different path for myself. Driven by a newfound determination, I conducted extensive research and made the decision to enrol in the CMA certification program offered by Simandhar. It was a pivotal step towards realizing my aspirations of forging a brighter future within the realm of finance.

Q. What were some of the sacrifices you had to make in your personal life while studying for the US CMA exams, and how did it feel when you finally achieved your goal?

On my path to becoming a CMA, I made significant sacrifices in terms of socializing with friends and attending family events. I devoted myself entirely to managing my studies and working from home. I meticulously structured my days and worked diligently to meet my targets. As the exam date drew nearer, my outings became increasingly scarce. In the final stretch leading up to the exam, I imposed even stricter limitations on my social activities. With a month left until the exam, I permitted myself to go out only once during the weekend, for a maximum of 3 to 4 hours, solely for the purpose of refreshing my mind. If the exam was scheduled for the current month, I remained at home for the entire duration.

The sense of accomplishment upon reaching my goal was beyond words. It served as a validation of the age-old adage: the harder the struggle, the sweeter the fruit. This sentiment is difficult to convey adequately in words.

Q. Can you share a story of someone who greatly influenced and supported you during your exam preparation, and how did their belief in you make a difference?

Throughout my exam preparation journey, my mother offered unwavering support. In moments of self-doubt, her reassurances echoed in my mind, urging me not to succumb to fear, as it would only impede my potential for success. Inspired by her strong belief in me, I committed myself wholeheartedly, pouring not just a 100, but 200 percent effort into achieving my goals. Her encouragement became the driving force behind my determination to excel.

Q. Can you share a funny moment that happened during your exam preparation that you still remember and laugh about?

In my pursuit of success, I frequently sought guidance from seniors who had overcome the challenges I faced. I reached out to them for insights, eager to develop my own strategies for success. Reflecting on those interactions now, I can't help but smile. Though my inquiries may have seemed bothersome at the time, their assistance was invaluable. Despite my numerous questions and potential inconveniences, their patience and unwavering support played a pivotal role in my journey to success.

Q. How has your achievement in passing the CMA exams inspired you to set higher goals and continue growing both personally and professionally?

Passing the CMA exam reinforced my belief in myself. Despite struggling with low self-esteem, achieving success in the exam in my first attempt instilled in me the confidence that I can accomplish anything in life through discipline and determination. This journey not only enhanced my discipline but also significantly bolstered my self-esteem.

Q. Can you recall a moment when you felt truly proud of your accomplishment in passing the exams, and how did that fuel your motivation to keep achieving more?

Despite lacking discipline during my school and college days, the level of hard work and dedication I invested in my exam preparation is a source of immense pride for me. This newfound discipline not only enabled me to succeed in the exam but also transformed me into a better professional overall. The memories of my preparation, during which I gave my utmost effort and achieved success, continue to inspire me as I set new goals in my life.

Q. How did Simandhar Education's supportive community and network of fellow students contribute to your motivation and success in passing the CMA exams and getting placed?

As previously mentioned, the seniors from Simandhar were instrumental in my journey. Their guidance and insights were invaluable, especially in shaping my exam strategies and ultimately contributing to my success. In particular, I am deeply grateful for

Sripal sir's advice on studying annual reports, analyzing earnings transcript calls, maintaining confidence, and embodying humility. His wisdom proved to be instrumental not only in my exam preparation but also in securing placements through successful interviews.

Q. What advice or message would you give to someone considering Simandhar Education as their CPA/CMA exam prep institute and seeking guidance from global CPA, CMA, EA instructor, Mr. Sripal Jain?

My advice to you is to wholeheartedly focus on your preparation and personal strategy to excel in the exam. Give it your all, and trust that Simandhar will provide the necessary opportunities and platforms for you to achieve your dreams. With access to top-notch study materials, unwavering faculty support, and excellent placement assistance, there's no need to worry if you're at Simandhar. Stay dedicated, stay focused, and success will surely follow.

Q. If Simandhar Education were to organize a reality TV show, what kind of challenges or tasks would it create for the contestants to test their accounting and finance skills?

Case studies and scenario analysis are powerful tools for testing and applying finance concepts in real-world contexts. By presenting students with realistic business scenarios, these exercises encourage critical thinking, problem-solving, and the practical application of theoretical knowledge.

Q. What is the best part about being a Simandhar student?

The standout feature about Simandhar is that it provides lifelong support for your career and learning journey, extending beyond course completion.

Q. How much has your life changed since the day you enrolled for the course?

It has transformed me completely, both professionally and personally. Professionally, I've grown significantly in discipline and confidence. Personally, I've embraced a mindset of helping others, a value instilled in me by Simandhar. While I may not have reached their level yet, I'm committed to continuous self-improvement.

Chapter 03

ON TOP OF THE WORLD

Introduction:

Following a known path may display bravery, but forging a new one requires even greater courage. Kavneet Hanspal, hailing from Delhi, initially contemplated pursuing a CA degree but ultimately chose to pursue a CPA, recognizing its greater value and prospects in the field of accounting. Despite the challenges and extra effort required, Kavneet boldly paved his own path toward the CPA designation, achieving not only success but also garnering recognition beyond his imagination. He was awarded the prestigious Elijah Watts Sells award for achieving the highest international score of 95.6.

Kavneet attributes his success to the unwavering support of his family, as well as the innovative approach and exceptional guidance provided by Simandhar Education. He acknowledges the pivotal role played by the mentors and trainers at Simandhar Education, who steered him in the right direction and ensured his success in not only attaining his goal but also topping the highly competitive and demanding CPA exams. His journey serves as a poignant reminder of the transformative power of determination, hard work, and a focused approach to both personal and professional aspirations.

Q&A with Kavneet:

Q: What inspired you to pursue a career in accounting and finance?

My father's profession as an accountant initially ignited my interest in the field. Despite having a natural inclination towards science, I found Chemistry less appealing as a subject. That is why I opted for Commerce with Mathematics as my high school stream. During those formative years, we had the privilege of hosting several Chartered Accountants who shared insights into their profession. Their experiences resonated with me, prompting me to pursue the CPA course. I love how the rules and systems of accounting ensure meticulous entering and recording of all business transactions where both sides of every transaction can be shown and balanced.

Q. What were some of the sacrifices you had to make in your personal life while studying for the US CPA exams, and how did it feel when you finally achieved your goal?

During my B. Com (Hons) course at Delhi University, I had lots of amazing friends and was always eager to participate in various events and festivities. However, once I began my CPA journey, I decided to seclude myself at home and prioritize my studies. The rigorous exam schedule demanded strict discipline and isolation from the outside world which was intensified by the onset of the COVID-19 pandemic. Despite the challenges, the joy and sense of relief on clearing my exams was beyond heartening. After over four years of dedication, I could achieve not only top scores but the prestigious Elijah Watt Sells award as well. That was the icing on the cake for me.

Q. Can you share a story of someone who greatly influenced and supported you during your exam preparation, and how did their belief in you make a difference?

My brother has always been my rock, offering both comfort and motivation throughout my CPA journey. Every morning we would speak for a while. I would share my study targets and progress, and he in turn helped alleviate my anxiety and kept me grounded. I also sought guidance from a senior friend who had previously aced the exams and who provided invaluable insights. But most important I feel was the encouragement and camaraderie fostered by Sripal sir and the Simandhar family that had truly instilled confidence and solidarity, making the journey relatable and inspiring.

Q. Can you share a funny moment that happened during your exam preparation that you still remember and laugh about?

One amusing memory from my exam preparations involves my nerves on the way to the exam center. Despite a one-hour journey, I'd be trembling with fear the entire time. To ease my anxiety, I'd call my brother, who was in the US where it was evening. Throughout the hour-long conversation, we'd intentionally steer clear of discussing studies or the impending exam. Instead, we'd share jokes, and stories, and simply make each other laugh, turning a nerve-wracking journey into a light-hearted bonding session.

Q. How has your achievement in passing the CPA exams inspired you to set higher goals and continue growing both personally and professionally?

Having passed the exams, I felt a renewed sense of purpose and accomplishment. I felt I could do more, achieve more and continue unafraid of learning greater things. Passing these tough exams truly boosted my confidence level, making me believe I could scale loftier learning goals. I now knew that I had both the discipline and the dedication to achieve whatever I set my mind to.

Q. Can you recall a moment when you felt truly proud of your accomplishment in passing the exams, and how did that fuel your motivation to keep achieving more?

I joined Ernst & Young as soon as the CPA results were declared. That was a milestone in my life that I will forever cherish. I remember how Anshu Rathore, a global leader at EY publicly acknowledged my achievement in one of the company – wide meets. It was a surreal and an extremely gratifying experience to be recognised by some of the important individuals and leaders of the company. That is how I was motivated to continue to strive for excellence in life.

Q. How did Simandhar Education's supportive community and network of fellow students contribute to your motivation and success in passing the CPA exams and getting placed?

Simandhar's inclusive community fosters a sense of belonging and support. Interacting with fellow students, alumni, and mentors created a conducive environment for learning and growth. The comprehensive support extended by Simandhar's placement team ensured a seamless transition into my dream job within a week of receiving my results.

Q. What advice or message would you give to someone considering Simandhar Education as their CPA exam prep institute and seeking guidance from global CPA, CMA, EA instructor, Mr. Sripal Jain?

For comprehensive support and guidance in pursuing professional courses, Simandhar is unparalleled. Sripal sir's unwavering dedication ensures holistic assistance from course enrollment to career advancement. If you aspire to succeed in the accounting field, Simandhar is the ideal choice.

Q. If Simandhar Education were to organize a reality TV show, what kind of challenges or tasks would it create for the contestants to test their accounting and finance skills?

The reality show could feature challenges like case studies, quiz rounds, and rapid-fire sessions, designed to test contestants' accounting and finance acumen under pressure.

Q. What is the best part about being a Simandhar student?

As a Simandhar student, the assurance of receiving top-notch resources and guidance, akin to studying in the USA, instills confidence and fosters professional growth.

Q. How much has your life changed since the day you enrolled for the course?

Enrolling in the course kickstarted a remarkable career journey, broadening my horizons and offering growth opportunities. From visiting EY offices in Boston and New York to engaging with partners over lunch/dinner, the course has opened doors to invaluable experiences and prospects.

Chapter 04

FROM SETBACK TO SUCCESS

Introduction:

Ordinary transforms into extraordinary not by chance or luck, but through sincere efforts, diligence, and unwavering determination.

Jigar Variyavwala exemplifies this truth. Having once made the tough decision to step away from pursuing CA, he boldly opted to seek the CPA qualification, knowing that it held greater challenges but believing it also had greater potential for a better future. He understood that the path to becoming a CPA would not be that easy, but easy has never been Jigar Variyavwala's approach. He demonstrated his mettle by not only successfully completing his CPA exams but also securing an impressive position at Deloitte.

Success is indeed a journey; a captivating and inspiring narrative, especially when told through the experiences of individuals like Jigar.

Q&A with Jigar:

Q: What inspired you to pursue a career in accounting and finance?

I am intrigued by how accounting and finance have evolved in the past 5-10 years, particularly the impact technological integrations have had on all organizational practices. I also recognize the need to be updated and aware of the numerous advancements in the fields of accounting and finance. I was impressed with the way AICPA, the world's renowned accounting body, has continually kept itself updated on market trends and technological innovations and has implemented those changes in its courses and curriculum. Taking up CPA thus seemed like a logical choice to ensure I remain at the forefront of industry development.

Q. What were some of the sacrifices you had to make in your personal life while studying for the US CPA exams, and how did it feel when you finally achieved your goal?

I had to make a significant shift in my routine as basically I am a night owl and had to adapt to an early morning regimen. I avoided family outings and social gatherings even on weekends to prioritize my CPA goal. However, the greatest reward came from witnessing the pride in my parents' eyes upon achieving my CPA designation – it meant everything to me.

Q. Can you share a story of someone who greatly influenced and supported you during your exam preparation, and how did their belief in you make a difference?

My best friend kept motivating me throughout my CPA course. He would encourage me and keep my spirits afloat whenever I was going through self-doubting moments. His belief in me and his unwavering support certainly gave me the much-needed impetus and confidence to carry on with my study schedule and pursue the course with determination.

Q. Can you share a funny moment that happened during your exam preparation that you still remember and laugh about?

I would often struggle to stay awake, especially during early morning CPA classes. During one such class, Sripal sir suddenly asked me a question on a topic I was clueless about. I was embarrassed, but the lesson I learned ensured that I stayed alert in all subsequent classes.

Q. How has your achievement of passing the CPA exams inspired you to set higher goals and continue growing both personally and professionally?

Completing my CPA exams instilled a newfound sense of confidence within me. This confidence enabled me to connect with individuals I once deemed intimidating and to expand my professional network. It also empowered me to interact confidently, even with esteemed leaders like the immediate Chair of AICPA, thus proving the positive impact of self-belief on personal growth and professional success.

Q. Can you recall a moment when you felt truly proud of your accomplishment in passing the exams, and how did that fuel your motivation to keep achieving more?

When I witness the kind of respect and admiration in people's eyes when I share my CPA achievement, I am filled with pride and a deep sense of gratitude. This kind of recognition keeps me humble and grateful as I continually strive for personal growth and professional ambitions.

Q. How did Simandhar Education's supportive community and network of fellow students contribute to your motivation and success in passing the CPA exams and getting placed?

Simandhar Education is not just a coaching institute; it is a community of like-minded students and aspirants. In the past two years, I have grown both personally and professionally in a supporting and encouraging environment led by our esteemed Sripal sir.

Q. What advice or message would you give to someone considering Simandhar Education as their CPA exam prep institute and seeking guidance from global CPA, CMA, EA instructor, Mr. Sripal Jain?

To all aspiring CPA/CMA/EA candidates, joining Simandhar Education isn't just about gaining course knowledge; it's about transforming into an well-rounded professional, capable of excelling in any corporate role or entrepreneurial venture, guided by the principles exemplified by Sripal sir.

Q. If Simandhar Education were to organize a reality TV show, what kind of challenges or tasks would it create for the contestants to test their accounting and finance skills?

Simandhar Education's reality TV show would focus on challenges testing contestants' conceptual understanding and ethical decision-making, fostering a holistic approach to accounting and finance skills.

Q. What is the best part about being a Simandhar student?

The best aspect of being a Simandhar student is belonging to a community that transcends traditional coaching institutes, fostering growth, collaboration, and a problem-solving mindset, rather than confining individuals to limited perspectives.

Q. How much has your life changed since the day you enrolled for the course?

Enrolling in Simandhar Education has fundamentally transformed my outlook on life. Beyond acquiring knowledge, it has taught me to approach challenges with a problem-solving mindset, shaping me into a more resilient and adaptable person prepared to navigate any situation.

Chapter 05

AGE IS A NUMBER, NOT A LIMITATION TO ACHIEVING SUCCESS

Introduction:

Defying societal expectations and challenging age-related stereotypes, Aparna Devalla stands out among her peers and contemporaries. By obtaining her CPA qualification at the age of 52, Aparna has demonstrated that age is merely a number, not a barrier to success and achievement. Her unwavering determination and resilience serve as a source of inspiration, particularly in an environment characterized by rigorous standards and fierce competition.

Navigating the demands of life and family, Aparna's journey is a testament to perseverance and optimism for those constrained by perceived limitations. Her attainment of a prestigious role as Senior Manager at Oremus underscores the timeless adage that it's never too late to pursue one's dreams and realize them.

Q&A with Aparna:

Q: What inspired you to pursue a career in accounting and finance?

I choose to pursue accountancy in school. Looking back, I am glad I did because I have grown to love and appreciate the real-world relevance of finance immensely. Finance plays an important role in all our lives, so having in-depth knowledge helps in problem-solving and addressing financial challenges.

Q. What were some of the sacrifices you had to make in your personal life while studying for the US CPA exams, and how did it feel when you finally achieved your goal?

During my CPA journey, I faced several difficult situations and health issues one after the other at home. I had to undergo a medical procedure. Then I had to serve as a primary caretaker to someone else at home. On top of all that I was racked with guilt at being unable to help my son who was facing a crisis in the US. But when I received my CPA results, I felt the struggles and adversities I went through during that time paid off and I could experience the full joy of the accomplishment. I did not allow the barriers of age or adversity to get in the way of my goal.

Q. Can you share a story of someone who greatly influenced and supported you during your exam preparation, and how did their belief in you make a difference?

Without hesitation or doubt, I would say that Sripal's unwavering belief in my abilities served as a constant source of encouragement during difficult times. Despite facing setbacks, his supportive words and guidance inspired me to persevere. Attending Sripal's seminars in Bangalore enabled me to connect with a supportive community, bolstering my resolve to overcome challenges. I must also acknowledge my husband's unwavering support throughout this journey.

Q. Can you share a funny moment that happened during your exam preparation that you still remember and laugh about?

One amusing incident occurred on my way to the exam center when a security guard mistook me for a parent waiting for their child and tried to prevent me from entering. It took some convincing to assure him that I was, in fact, there to write the exam, not waiting for someone else!

Q. How has your achievement in passing the CPA exams inspired you to set higher goals and continue growing both personally and professionally?

Passing the CPA exams has propelled me onto a new career path in US taxation, offering me opportunities for personal and professional growth over the next two decades. Instead of retiring, I've embraced a new challenge, fueling my ambition to continue learning and advancing in my field.

Q. Can you recall a moment when you felt truly proud of your accomplishment in passing the exams, and how did that fuel your motivation to keep achieving more?

Clearing my first exam, FAR, after a hiatus of 30 years since my last successful exam of ICWA, filled me with immense pride and satisfaction. This milestone moment fuelled my determination to persist and achieve further success in my CPA journey.

Q. How did Simandhar Education's supportive community and network of fellow students contribute to your motivation and success in passing the CPA exams and getting placed?

Simandhar's supportive community played a crucial role in keeping me motivated throughout my CPA journey, especially during periods of hiatus. Interacting with fellow students provided encouragement; and the leads provided by Simandhar ultimately led to my current employment.

Q. What advice or message would you give to someone considering Simandhar Education as their CPA exam prep institute and seeking guidance from global CPA, CMA, EA instructor, Mr. Sripal Jain?

Choosing Simandhar Education means choosing a dedicated institute committed to nurturing a community of professionals. With a comprehensive ecosystem and unwavering support, students receive the guidance and resources needed to achieve their goals, often leading to placement opportunities upon enrolment.

Q. What is the best part about being a Simandhar student?

Despite being in my fifties, being a Simandhar student has allowed me to embrace the student mindset once again, fostering continuous learning and growth regardless of age.

Q. How much has your life changed since the day you enrolled for the course?

Enrolling in the course paved the way for a new career path in US taxation, fundamentally transforming my life and offering avenues for personal and professional development that I had not previously imagined.

Chapter 06

A LEAP OF FAITH; A HEAP OF POSSIBILITIES

Introduction:

Taking a leap of faith can sometimes profoundly reshape the course of life, as it did for Srinivas Choppakatla. His decision to embark on the journey of the EA exams not only transformed his professional trajectory but also enriched his personal life. Srinivas's achievement in passing the exams and securing a full-time position at Oremus stands as a testament to his steadfast determination and relentless pursuit of success. Simandhar Education played a pivotal role in inspiring and supporting Srinivas, empowering him to pursue his aspirations and continually strive for growth, both professionally and personally.

Q&A with Srinivas:

Q: What inspired you to pursue a career in accounting and finance?

The wide range of career opportunities in accounting and finance was the primary motivator for me. The demand and growth prospects in this field surpass those of many others, making it an apt choice.

Q. What were some of the sacrifices you had to make in your personal life while studying for the US TAX – EA exams, and how did it feel when you finally achieved your goal?

During my exam preparation, I had to forgo several planned trips with friends, refrain from entertainment activities, and sacrifice leisure time, including playing cricket on weekends. Despite these sacrifices, achieving my goal brought immense joy not only to me but also to my family, who were elated with the positive impact it had on my life.

Q. Can you share a story of someone who greatly influenced and supported you during your exam preparation, and how did their belief in you make a difference?

My elder sister played a significant role in motivating and supporting me throughout my exam preparation journey. Despite facing personal challenges after our mother's passing, she assumed a maternal role and encouraged me to pursue various courses. Her unwavering support inspired me to focus on taxation, my area of interest, and become an EA.

Q. Can you share a funny moment that happened during your exam preparation that you still remember and laugh about?

A comical incident occurred just a week before my exams when, in a state of exhaustion, I woke up suddenly at 1:30 in the morning with my mind racing about exam preparation. Despite having studied diligently all day, I found myself attending a lecture on my phone while lying in bed. It was a humorous moment amid the intensity of exam preparation.

Q. How has your achievement in passing the EA exams inspired you to set higher goals and continue growing both personally and professionally?

Clearing the EA exams opened up numerous opportunities for me, prompting me to set higher goals and strive for personal and professional growth. The sense of accomplishment fuelled my motivation to pursue loftier objectives and embark on new challenges with confidence.

Q. Can you recall a moment when you felt truly proud of your accomplishment in passing the exams, and how did that fuel your motivation to keep achieving more?

Passing the EA exams filled me with immense pride, particularly because it marked a significant milestone in my unconventional career path. The experience of overcoming challenges and achieving success motivated me to push my boundaries further. Encouraged by the beauty of my journey thus far, I am now driven to challenge myself by undertaking more demanding courses, proving my capabilities, and ultimately achieving my long-term aspirations. I eagerly anticipate what lies ahead.

Q. How did Simandhar Education's supportive community and network of fellow students contribute to your motivation and success in passing the EA exams and getting placed?

Simandhar Education's supportive community and knowledgeable faculty played a crucial role in my exam preparation journey. Their expertise made complex topics approachable, and their encouragement boosted my confidence. Additionally, their assistance in placement soon after clearing one exam was invaluable, especially during challenging times like the COVID-19 pandemic.

Q. What advice or message would you give to someone considering Simandhar Education as their EA exam prep institute and seeking guidance from global CPA, CMA, EA instructor, Mr. Sripal Jain?

I wholeheartedly recommend Simandhar Education to anyone considering it for CPA, CMA or EA instructor exam preparation. Their exceptional track record in placements and course success rates sets them apart, and their commitment to transforming opportunities into reality is commendable. Under the guidance of Mr. Sripal Jain, students are not only provided with expert instruction but also empowered to achieve their dreams. Credit goes to Sripal sir for his remarkable capability in actualizing these opportunities, enabling us to live out our dreams while others can only envision them. His visionary leadership and commitment to student success are evident in the institute's unparalleled achievements. I am truly grateful for the invaluable support and guidance provided by Simandhar Education, and I am confident that others will benefit immensely from their expertise as well.

Q. If Simandhar Education were to organize a reality TV show, what kind of challenges or tasks would it create for the contestants to test their accounting and finance skills?

The reality TV show could feature challenges such as analyzing case laws and completing practical tax form filings to test the contestants' accounting and finance skills effectively.

Q. What is the best part about being a Simandhar student?

One of the most rewarding aspects of being a Simandhar student is the strong sense of community and support received from peers and faculty. The Telegram study groups serve as invaluable resources for collaboration, knowledge sharing, and mutual encouragement, ensuring that no student feels alone in their academic journey.

Q. How much has your life changed since the day you enrolled for the course?

Enrolling in the course and passing the EA exams has brought about a significant transformation in my life. I have become more confident, positive, and have improved in my communication skills. This achievement has not only enhanced my professional capabilities but has also positively impacted various aspects of my personal growth.

Chapter 07

SCORING & SECURING SUCCESS IN RIGHT STEPS

Introduction:

Everyone harbors dreams, but it's our actions that differentiate us. After graduating with a B.Com degree, Vaishnavi Patel set her sights on becoming a CPA. Her choice to enroll in Simandhar Education proved to be fruitful as she not only passed the CPA exams but also landed her dream role in the Merger & Acquisition department at Infosys.

Q&A with Vaishnavi:

Q: What inspired you to pursue a career in accounting and finance?

Accounting and finance have always intrigued me since my days as a commerce student. The blend of mathematics and analytical skills inherent in this field appealed to me.

Q. What were some of the sacrifices you had to make in your personal life while studying for the US CPA exams, and how did it feel when you finally achieved your goal?

To earn any professional degree, sacrifices in personal life are inevitable. I had to decline invitations from friends and family for outings, limit my social interactions when my study targets weren't met, and even forgo celebrating festivals until I reached my goal. However, when I finally cleared the CPA exams, it was a moment of immense joy as I could return to my personal life with a sense of accomplishment.

Q. Can you share a story of someone who greatly influenced and supported you during your exam preparation, and how did their belief in you make a difference?

During a particularly stressful period of non-stop studying, I confided in a peer from Simandhar who had experienced similar challenges. Her empathetic understanding and simple advice to take a short break to rejuvenate and regain focus helped me a lot.

Q. Can you share a funny moment that happened during your exam preparation that you still remember and laugh about?

While there were many funny moments during my study sessions, one that stands out is Sripal Sir's knack for bringing humor into our classes or events. His jokes not only lightened the atmosphere but also made learning incredibly enjoyable.

Q. How has your achievement in passing the CPA exams inspired you to set higher goals and continue growing both personally and professionally?

Becoming a CPA has instilled in me the desire to continually expand and deepen my knowledge to bring out the best in myself.

Q. Can you recall a moment when you felt truly proud of your accomplishment in passing the exams, and how did that fuel your motivation to keep achieving more?

Passing the Audit paper within a tight two-month deadline was a proud moment for me. It inspired me to tackle the rest of the papers promptly, driven by the goal of attaining the CPA title.

Q. How did Simandhar Education's supportive community and network of fellow students contribute to your motivation and success in passing the CPA exams and getting placed?

The supportive community and groups at Simandhar were instrumental in keeping me motivated throughout my CPA journey. Witnessing others pass their exams encouraged and reinforced my determination to clear my papers swiftly.

Q. What advice or message would you give to someone considering Simandhar Education as their CPA exam prep institute and seeking guidance from global CPA, CMA, EA instructor, Mr. Sripal Jain?

Without hesitation, I highly recommend joining Simandhar Education. Sripal sir and his team have ensured that I secured the profile I desired, and their support was invaluable in achieving it. The opportunity to secure an M&A profile at Infosys is a testament to Simandhar's dedication to student success.

Q. If Simandhar Education were to organize a reality TV show, what kind of challenges or tasks would it create for the contestants to test their accounting and finance skills?

Simandhar Education could organize mock exams and interviews to test contestants' financial and analytical skills, making it an engaging and insightful experience.

Q. What is the best part about being a Simandhar student?

The best part about being a Simandhar student is that they celebrate your success as their own, fostering a supportive and encouraging environment.

Q. How much has your life changed since the day you enrolled for the course?

Since enrolling and completing my CPA, I've gained more confidence, patience, analytical skills, and, of course, the professional designation that comes with it. It's been a transformative journey both personally and professionally.

Chapter 08

STRUGGLES AND SACRIFICES DETERMINE SUCCESS

Introduction:

Bobby Agarwal's journey from an employee of Standard Chartered Bank to the role of Assistant Vice President (AVP) at Citi Bank is one of determination, sacrifice, and triumph. Driven by ambition and tenacity, she embarked on the challenging path of becoming a CPA after completing her CA. In her reflective narrative, Bobby shares insights into the preparation process, highlighting the sacrifices made and the consistent support received from Simandhar Education. She attributes her personal and professional achievements to her perseverance and strong belief in the education system provided by Simandhar Education.

Q&A with Bobby:

Q: What inspired you to pursue a career in accounting and finance?

My inherent curiosity and questioning mind led me to choose a career in accounting and finance. Starting with accounting and now in internal audit at an investment bank, this career path allows me to fuel my curiosity daily, add value to organizations, challenge the status quo, and improve systems for the better.

Q. What were some of the sacrifices you had to make in your personal life while studying for the US CPA exams, and how did it feel when you finally achieved your goal?

During my CPA exam preparation, sacrifices were plentiful. I forwent vacations, missed spending time with friends and family, and even dedicated festival time to studying. Despite these sacrifices, I have no regrets. Each sacrifice was a step toward achieving my goals, and upon finally passing the exams, I felt a profound sense of pride and accomplishment.

Q. Can you share a story of someone who greatly influenced and supported you during your exam preparation, and how did their belief in you make a difference?

Throughout my CPA journey, my fellow students-turned-friends from the Simandhar CPA batch provided unwavering support. Their belief in my abilities, encouragement during challenging times, and camaraderie made the journey memorable, easier, and achievable.

Q. Can you share a funny moment that happened during your exam preparation that you still remember and laugh about?

During our exam preparation, Simandhar organized a Halloween event where we had to come up with a group name. The plethora of hilarious name choices sparked laughter and made it difficult to choose just one.

Q. How has your achievement in passing the CPA exams inspired you to set higher goals and continue growing both personally and professionally?

Passing the CPA exams taught me that learning is a lifelong journey. It instilled in me the importance of embracing challenges, maintaining a positive outlook, and continuously expanding my knowledge to excel both professionally and personally.

Q. Can you recall a moment when you felt truly proud of your accomplishment in passing the exams, and how did that fuel your motivation to keep achieving more?

Passing two CPA papers simultaneously while balancing a demanding full-time job was a defining moment for me. It showcased my potential and shattered self-imposed limitations, fueling my belief that anything is achievable with the right mindset and approach.

Q. How did Simandhar Education's supportive community and network of fellow students contribute to your motivation and success in passing the CPA exams and getting placed?

The supportive community and network of fellow students at Simandhar were instrumental in keeping me motivated and focused throughout my CPA journey. Their encouragement, support, and shared experiences made the challenging journey more manageable and enjoyable.

Q. What advice or message would you give to someone considering Simandhar Education as their CPA exam prep institute and seeking guidance from global CPA, CMA, EA instructor, Mr. Sripal Jain?

Choosing Simandhar Education means choosing a supportive environment led by genuine mentors like Sripal Jain. His honesty, commitment to student growth, and strong values make Simandhar an excellent choice for CPA exam preparation.

Q. If Simandhar Education were to organize a reality TV show, what kind of challenges or tasks would it create for the contestants to test their accounting and finance skills?

Simandhar Education could organize challenges like naming top finance leaders in the industry or counting backward from one million while identifying the number of zeros in a trillion—a humorous yet insightful way to test accounting and finance skills.

Q. What is the best part about being a Simandhar student?

The most rewarding part of being a Simandhar student is the relationships built with teachers, fellow students, and mentors. The supportive community fosters personal and professional growth, making the journey memorable and impactful.

Q. How much has your life changed since the day you enrolled for the course?

Enrolling in the course has unlocked my potential, built lasting friendships, and introduced me to great leaders. Professionally, it has strengthened my foundational beliefs, inspired me to be a better person and leader, and fueled my continuous learning journey. Overall, it's been a transformative experience both personally and professionally.

Chapter 09

UNEXPECTED TURNS TO ENDLESS POSSIBILITIES

Introduction:

The journey to success often takes unexpected turns, marked by setbacks and failures that ultimately shape a unique path. Those who navigate such paths are anything but ordinary; they possess the resilience and determination to carve out a unique route to success.

Despite facing a setback in his pursuit of CA, Surya Teja remained undeterred, using it as fuel to forge ahead on his journey. Qualifying as a CPA through Simandhar Education opened doors to a world brimming with endless possibilities. From securing an internship at Citrin

Cooperation Inc. to landing a full-time position at EY, and culminating in an overseas placement at SPA Associates Michigan, USA, Surya Teja's success knew no bounds.

Q&A with Surya Teja:

Q: What inspired you to pursue a career in accounting and finance?

My passion for numbers at a young age and consistently excelling in mathematics during my school years fueled my decision to pursue a career in accounting.

Q. What were some of the sacrifices you had to make in your personal life while studying for the US CPA exams, and how did it feel when you finally achieved your goal?

Sacrificing leisure activities like hanging out with friends and going to movies was necessary to prioritize my CPA studies. However, upon completion the sense of relief was immense, and I re-joined these activities with newfound enthusiasm.

Q. Can you share a story of someone who greatly influenced and supported you during your exam preparation, and how did their belief in you make a difference?

Sripal Sir's staunch belief in me, especially during the transition from pursuing CA to CPA, was pivotal. His dedication to continuous learning and pursuit of dreams inspired me to work diligently, shaping my journey to where I am today.

Q. Can you share a funny moment that happened during your exam preparation that you still remember and laugh about?

Aiding newly enrolled students with their CPA queries, while jokingly considering myself part of the Simandhar faculty, always brought a smile to my face.

Q. How has your achievement in passing the CPA exams inspired you to set higher goals and continue growing both personally and professionally?

Passing the CPA exams not only secured a job at a Big 4 firm in India but also instilled confidence to pursue my dream of working in the US. The recognition and respect earned through this achievement motivated me to aim higher.

Q. Can you recall a moment when you felt truly proud of your accomplishment in passing the exams, and how did that fuel your motivation to keep achieving more?

I vividly recall the moment when I passed my last section. It was truly a remarkable landmark because it signified to everyone, including myself, that I was no longer a failure. Witnessing the joy on my loved ones' faces reinforced my determination to pursue further success.

Q. How did Simandhar Education's supportive community and network of fellow students contribute to your motivation and success in passing the CPA exams and getting placed?

While I derived much of my inspiration from Sripal Sir, numerous other resources played a crucial role in helping me and every student achieve our goals. Networking was among the most significant factors, and the Telegram groups for each section provided us with confidence that we were not missing out on anything.

Q. What advice or message would you give to someone considering Simandhar Education as their CPA exam prep institute and seeking guidance from global CPA, CMA, EA instructor, Mr. Sripal Jain?

Four words…" just go for it!"

Q. If Simandhar Education were to organize a reality TV show, what kind of challenges or tasks would it create for the contestants to test their accounting and finance skills?

I believe Simandhar would create live practical scenarios to test contestants' accounting and finance skills, pushing them beyond boundaries.

Q. What is the best part about being a Simandhar student?

The genuine support and affection received from everyone around.

Q. How much has your life changed since the day you enrolled for the course?

Enrolling at Simandhar marked a significant turning point, guiding me from being a CA dropout to achieving CPA certification and expanding my horizons from India to the USA.

Chapter 10

AGAINST ALL ODDS

Introduction:

The inspiring journey of Bhawna Jain stands as a testament to the resilience and determination required to pursue one's dreams against all odds. Transitioning from an M. Com graduate to a devoted housewife for 17 years, Bhawna's remarkable path to becoming a qualified CPA sets her apart from her peers. With a background in finance and accounting, she tackled the rigorous challenges of the US CPA exams, showcasing unparalleled sacrifice, perseverance, and eventual triumph. Bhawna is a testament to the transformative power of education and the invaluable support provided by Simandhar Education on her journey to success.

Q&A with Bhawna Jain:

Q: What inspired you to pursue a career in accounting and finance?

I was passionate about pursuing a professional degree in finance, having completed both my graduation and post-graduation in Finance and Accounting.

Q. What were some of the sacrifices you had to make in your personal life while studying for the US CPA exams, and how did it feel when you finally achieved your goal?

Sacrificing my family and personal time over one and a half years was necessary to complete my CPA. However, the pride I felt upon seeing the results of my last exam was truly fulfilling.

Q. Can you share a story of someone who greatly influenced and supported you during your exam preparation, and how did their belief in you make a difference?

Upon joining Simandhar, the success stories of fellow students greatly influenced me, keeping me motivated throughout my journey.

Q. How has your achievement in passing the CPA exams inspired you to set higher goals and continue growing both personally and professionally?

Completing my CPA opened doors to opportunities with prestigious organizations, and I now aspire to work as a freelancer, continuously aiming for growth.

Q. Can you recall a moment when you felt truly proud of your accomplishment in passing the exams, and how did that fuel your motivation to keep achieving more?

Clearing all exams in one shot boosted my confidence, especially after being a housewife for 17 years. It instilled in me the drive to strive for further accomplishments.

Q. How did Simandhar Education's supportive community and network of fellow students contribute to your motivation and success in passing the CPA exams and getting placed?

It was an amazing journey with Simandhar. The real-time query resolution on the Telegram groups was immensely helpful. Simandhar provides excellent lectures and faculty support to students.

Q. What advice or message would you give to someone considering Simandhar Education as their CPA exam prep institute and seeking guidance from global CPA, CMA, EA instructor, Mr. Sripal Jain?

Simandhar is unquestionably an excellent institute to join as it offers real-time support from document evaluation to exam clearance. Their placement support is undoubtedly top-notch. In my case, securing my job wouldn't have been possible without the personal efforts of Sripal sir, especially considering I had been a housewife for 17 years.

Q. If Simandhar Education were to organize a reality TV show, what kind of challenges or tasks would it create for the contestants to test their accounting and finance skills?

Challenges focusing on mastering the basics of accounting and finance would be ideal for testing contestants' skills.

Q. What is the best part about being a Simandhar student?

The sense of camaraderie among fellow students, the mentorship provided by faculty members, and the guidance from Mr. Sripal Jain make the journey truly enriching.

Q. How much has your life changed since the day you enrolled for the course?

Enrolling in the course marked a significant transformation in both my personal and professional life, propelling me toward new heights of success and fulfillment.

Chapter 11

UNVEILING THE PATH TO PROFESSIONAL SUCCESS

Introduction:

Knowledge serves as the foundation upon which our aspirations are built, offering pathways to endless possibilities. For Shrikesh Lahoti, this axiom rings true as he embarked on a journey fuelled by ambition and guided by the pursuit of excellence in education. From the halls of Simandhar Education to the bustling corridors of Accenture, Shrikesh's determination, coupled with the right guidance and exceptional mentorship, propelled him forward. With single-minded dedication, he embraced the pursuit of knowledge, recognizing Simandhar Education as the catalyst for attaining his CPA qualification and paving the way for his professional success. Through his story, we witness the transformative power of education and the profound impact it can have on shaping one's future.

Q&A with Shrikesh Lahoti:

Q: What inspired you to pursue a career in accounting and finance?

Growing up in a business-oriented family environment, Accounting and Finance always interested me. Witnessing how financial data could be harnessed to drive informed decisions and fuel business success fascinated me deeply. This fascination spurred me to pursue courses like CA and CPA, igniting a passion for leveraging numbers to create impactful strategies.

Q. What were some of the sacrifices you had to make in your personal life while studying for the US CPA exams, and how did it feel when you finally achieved your goal?

Sacrificing personal milestones like birthdays, family gatherings, and leisure time with friends became inevitable to excel in my CPA studies. Yet the pride reflected in my parents' eyes upon my exam success eclipsed any sacrifices made. Their joy and validation of my hard work made every sacrifice worthwhile, marking a deeply fulfilling achievement.

Q. Can you share a story of someone who greatly influenced and supported you during your exam preparation, and how their belief in you made a difference?

In 2018, I had an important conversation with Sripal sir. Though I wasn't yet enrolled with Simandhar Education, his constant support during my CA preparations proved invaluable. Whenever I faced academic challenges, his guidance and encouragement fuelled my determination, significantly contributing to my exam success.

Q. Can you share a funny moment that happened during your exam preparation that you still remember and laugh about?

During my CA coaching classes in Pune, I once dozed off and was caught by the professor. To lighten the mood, he asked me to sing a song, which I did with a comically awful rendition, eliciting laughter from the entire class. Such moments provided much-needed levity amidst the rigors of exam preparation.

Q. How has your achievement in passing the CPA exams inspired you to set higher goals and continue growing both personally and professionally?

Initially daunting, my journey towards CPA certification became a testament to the transformative power of proper guidance and support. With Simandhar Education's effective assistance, I cleared my exams in just 8 months, reaffirming that with determination and mentorship, any goal is within reach. This achievement instilled in me the confidence to aspire for greater milestones, culminating in my decision to pursue an MS in Accounting from the esteemed University of Washington.

Q. Can you recall a moment when you felt truly proud of your accomplishment in passing the exams, and how did that fuel your motivation to keep achieving more?

A defining moment came when a US partner visited our office, and I proudly introduced myself as a CA CPA. Witnessing his genuine happiness and surprise at my achievements at a young age filled me with immense pride. This encounter served as a powerful reminder of the possibilities that lie ahead, propelling me to pursue even loftier aspirations.

Q. How did Simandhar Education's supportive community and network of fellow students contribute to your motivation and success in passing the CPA exams and getting placed?

Enrolling with Simandhar unveiled the significance of networking in professional growth. Being part of this community introduced me to diverse individuals, enabling interactions with professionals from multinational corporations and hearing inspiring success stories. The invaluable support and guidance provided through platforms like Telegram and alumni groups played a vital role in my interview preparations and eventual placement at Deloitte, fulfilling my career aspirations.

Q. What advice or message would you give someone considering Simandhar Education as their CPA exam prep institute and seeking guidance from global CPA, CMA, EA instructor, Mr. Sripal Jain?

My advice is simple: entrust your future to Simandhar Education. Mr. Sripal Jain's dedication to student success is unparalleled. His commitment extends beyond enrolled students, exemplifying a genuine passion for nurturing talent and contributing to the larger student community.

Q. What is the best part about being a Simandhar student?

The most gratifying aspect of being a Simandhar student is the extensive network it offers. The institute's personalized approach treats each student with utmost care, providing comprehensive support throughout the journey. From resolving queries to offering strategic exam preparation assistance, Simandhar ensures every student receives individualized attention, fostering a conducive environment for growth and success.

Q. How much has your life changed since the day you enrolled for the course?

Enrolling with Simandhar Education marked a significant turning point in my life. With their support, I effortlessly completed the CPA certification and secured a position at my dream company, Deloitte. Now, armed with their guidance, I am poised to embark on a new chapter, pursuing an MS in Accounting from the University of Washington in the United States.

Chapter 12

BREAKING RECORDS – THE YOUNGEST CPA WORLD TOPPER

Introduction:

Success in the competitive finance and accounting world demands nothing less than diligent effort, discipline, and hard work. Who knows this better than Khusbhu Mittal, who has not only etched her name as the youngest CPA world topper but also earned the prestigious Elijah Watt Sells Award in 2023. Her exceptional achievement stands as a testament to her dedication and outstanding performance. Her inspiring journey is bound to leave you in awe and admiration.

Q&A with Khusbhu:

Q: What inspired you to pursue a career in accounting and finance?

During my schooling years, my passion for mathematics and problem-solving led me to choose commerce, although I soon discovered that accounting differed significantly from mathematics. Surprisingly, I developed a deep appreciation for accounting as a subject during my B.Com (Hons.) studies. It was during this time that I realized my interest in pursuing a career related to accounting, taxation, finance, or similar fields. Inspired by my brother, who was pursuing CA, I decided to build a long-term career in this domain. His recommendation to pursue the US CPA qualification resonated with me as it promised global opportunities and a shorter completion time compared to CA. Already midway through college, opting for the CPA route proved to be the perfect decision, and I am grateful for my brother's guidance.

Q. What were some of the sacrifices you had to make in your personal life while studying for the US CPA exams, and how did it feel when you finally achieved your goal?

I had to forgo many family functions, festivals, office events, and gatherings with friends while studying for the CPA exams. Additionally, I missed my M. Com exams due to illness and had to prioritize my CPA studies. While I wouldn't classify these as sacrifices per se, they are moments I wish I could have experienced. Balancing work and studies were challenging, causing many personal activities to be put on hold. However, looking back now, I realize that the effort was worth it. The sense of happiness, relief, and pride upon passing one of the world's most prestigious professional courses is unparalleled.

Q. Can you share a story of someone who greatly influenced and supported you during your exam preparation, and how did their belief in you make a difference?

I've been fortunate to receive support from numerous people throughout this journey, making it challenging to single out just one. However, if I were to highlight someone, it would be my close friend, Gunjan. Before I embarked on my CPA journey, Gunjan lent me her books, aiding me in making the decision to pursue CPA. Once I committed to the path and enrolled for the exams, she became my guiding light every step of the way. From outlining the timeline to suggesting the sequence for taking the exams, Gunjan offered invaluable assistance. During moments of doubt or when my confidence wavered, she remained a steadfast source of belief and support. Her encouragement and countless acts of kindness have left an indelible mark, for which I'll forever be grateful.

Q. Can you share a funny moment that happened during your exam preparation that you still remember and laugh about?

During my CPA preparation, I had an interesting relationship with social media apps, particularly Instagram. I made a conscious decision to keep the app uninstalled most of the time to minimize distractions. However, there was one incident that stood out. A friend used a trendy phrase in our conversation, which I misunderstood and took to heart, leading to a few days of unnecessary upset. It turned out that the phrase was part of Instagram slang at that time. Reflecting on this misunderstanding later, I found humor in the situation. Despite occasional lapses into FOMO (Fear of Missing Out), where I would reinstall Instagram briefly to catch up on updates before uninstalling it again, has become a light-hearted story that I can now laugh about.

Q. How has your achievement in passing the CPA exams inspired you to set higher goals and continue growing both personally and professionally?

Now that I've successfully passed the CPA exams, I find myself with ample time to devote to both personal and professional growth. This achievement has infused me with a newfound sense of positivity and a determined attitude to seize opportunities. Looking ahead to 2024, my professional goals involve delivering high-quality work and advancing within the firm. On a personal level, I aim to prioritize my well-being by dedicating at least 150 minutes per week to physical activity, honing my skills in pilates, yoga, and cooking. Additionally, I aspire to enrich my mind by reading 5 to 6 books throughout the year. These goals reflect my commitment to continuous improvement and holistic development in all aspects of life.

Q. Can you recall a moment when you felt truly proud of your accomplishment in passing the exams, and how did that fuel your motivation to keep achieving more?

When I sat for my first exam, FAR, I was filled with a mix of nervousness and excitement, unsure of what to expect in terms of difficulty or outcome. It was a feeling I believe many experienced during their inaugural exam. Despite the uncertainty, I committed myself wholeheartedly to both the preparation and execution of the test. Exiting the prometric center afterward, I found myself with a singular thought: "I couldn't have given any more. Now, it's in the hands of fate." Weeks later, as I awaited the results, I was met with a remarkable sight: a perfect score of 99, a rare feat in the realm of CPA exams. In that moment, a surge of pride washed over me, igniting a fire to strive for even greater heights. It was a profound lesson learned – that diligent effort and dedication are the truest paths to success, with rewards sure to follow suit.

Q. How did Simandhar Education's supportive community and network of fellow students contribute to your motivation and success in passing the CPA exams and getting placed?

When undertaking the rigorous journey of pursuing a challenging degree like CPA, it's not uncommon to feel isolated at times. While friends and family offer support, there's a unique need for companions who understand the exact trials and triumphs you're experiencing. In this regard, Simandhar Education has excelled in fostering a vibrant community of learners, providing invaluable support and motivation. Their Telegram groups serve as dynamic platforms where doubts are swiftly resolved, and fellow aspirants freely share exam experiences and strategies. Engaging with this supportive network proved instrumental in my exam success, underscoring the immense value of camaraderie in such pursuits.

Q. What advice or message would you give someone considering Simandhar Education as their CPA exam prep institute and seeking guidance from global CPA, CMA, EA instructor, Mr. Sripal Jain?

If you're considering enrolling in a course at Simandhar, my advice is simple: don't hesitate—just do it. From the initial steps like evaluation processes and obtaining the NTS to placements and licensure, Simandhar provides comprehensive support throughout your journey. With their guidance, you can focus wholeheartedly on your studies. Moreover, don't hesitate to seek counsel from Mr. Sripal Jain, whose extensive experience spanning over a decade in finance and accounting makes him an invaluable resource. Personally, during my exam preparation, I was feeling nervous, so I reached out to him directly. His insightful study tips proved pivotal to my success, underscoring the immense value of his mentorship.

Q. If Simandhar Education were to organize a reality TV show, what kind of challenges or tasks would it create for the contestants to test their accounting and finance skills?

If Simandhar Education were to organize a reality TV show, they could design challenges to test contestants' accounting and finance skills through various activities such as a rapid-fire round with accounting and finance questions, guessing accounting terms from definitions, examples, or memes, creating dummy stocks, and tasks like creating investment portfolios. These challenges would not only gauge their theoretical knowledge but also their practical application and analytical skills in real-world financial scenarios.

Q. What is the best part about being a Simandhar student?

The best part about being a Simandhar student is undoubtedly the sense of belonging to a community of like-minded individuals.

Q. How much has your life changed since the day you enrolled for the course?

Since the day I enrolled for the course, my life has undergone significant changes. Most notably, I have become more disciplined in various aspects of life. This journey has imparted several valuable life lessons, among which is the profound teaching from the Bhagavad Gita: "You have the right to work, but not to the fruits of work." This philosophy resonates deeply with me, and I intend to abide by it indefinitely.

Chapter 13

FROM CA TO WORLD US CPA TOPPER IN LESS THAN A YEAR

Introduction:

A recipient of the prestigious Elijah Watt Sells Award, Dhurv Patel has carved a path of excellence by achieving remarkable scores and securing a coveted placement at one of the Big4 accounting firms, Ernst & Young (EY), immediately following the announcement of his CPA results. Despite already being a qualified CA, Dhurv recognized the importance of obtaining a globally recognized certification to meet the demands of the market. Hence, he decided to pursue the CPA credential through Simandhar Education. Remarkably, Dhurv completed all four sections of the CPA course in an astonishingly short period of around 10 months. He diligently attended every lecture, completed every set of MCQs, and engaged with every recommended simulation as part of his exam preparation regimen. Dhurv's outstanding scores stand as a testament to the undeniable truth that hard work yields remarkable results.

Q&A with Dhruv Patel:

Q: What inspired you to pursue a career in accounting and finance?

Interestingly, my journey into accounting began with the process of elimination. Upon completing my 10th grade, I was determined to pursue a course other than engineering. This left me with two major options: Medicine (Doctor) or Commerce. Considering the lengthy duration required for medical studies, I opted for Commerce, which eventually led me to pursue a career in accounting.

Q. What were some of the sacrifices you had to make in your personal life while studying for the US CPA exams, and how did it feel when you finally achieved your goal?

Embarking on the journey toward any professional qualification necessitates considerable time and dedication, a lesson I learned during my CA days. Upon initiating my CPA journey, I made the tough decision to resign from my rewarding position at a leading private sector bank to fully commit to CPA preparation. This commitment demanded long hours of consistent study every day. However, upon clearing the CPA exams, every sacrifice felt justified, and the sense of accomplishment was immensely rewarding.

Q. Can you share a story of someone who greatly influenced and supported you during your exam preparation, and how did their belief in you make a difference?

During my exam preparation, my sister Kinjal Sheth played a pivotal role. She was the one who initially encouraged me to pursue CPA in the first place. Throughout the journey, she provided support, always available to talk even during odd hours. I can confidently say that she served as both my mental and financial backbone throughout my CPA journey.

Q. Can you share a funny moment that happened during your exam preparation that you still remember and laugh about?

Though not a funny incident, one particular moment from my exam preparation still brings a smile to my face whenever I think about it. Just three weeks before my final paper FAR exam, I fell ill and was admitted to the hospital due to dengue fever. While lying on the hospital bed, all I could think about was whether I would be able to pass the exam or not. However, with the grace of God, I managed to clear the exam with a score of 98. Looking back, I smile and am reminded that every effort we put into pursuing our goals count, regardless of the challenges we face.

Q. How has your achievement in passing the CPA exams inspired you to set higher goals and continue growing both personally and professionally?

Passing the CPA exams was a significant achievement, but receiving the Elijah Watt Sells Award elevated my confidence to new heights. This recognition instilled in me a belief that setting ambitious goals is not only possible but essential for personal and professional growth. It taught me that with persistent effort and dedication, even the loftiest aspirations can be realized. Thus, my achievement in the CPA exams has inspired me to set even higher goals and continue striving for excellence in all aspects of my life.

Q. Can you recall a moment when you felt truly proud of your accomplishment in passing the exams, and how did that fuel your motivation to keep achieving more?

Achieving a score of 98 on the first paper of BEC was a moment of immense pride and satisfaction for me. It served as validation for the hard work and dedication I had put into my exam preparation. This accomplishment fueled my motivation to continue striving for excellence in the remaining papers. It showed me that with perseverance and determination, I could achieve outstanding results, reinforcing my belief in my abilities and inspiring me to push even harder to excel in the subsequent exams.

Q. How did Simandhar Education's supportive community and network of fellow students contribute to your motivation and success in passing the CPA exams and getting placed?

The supportive community and network of fellow students at Simandhar Education played a vital role in my journey to passing the CPA exams and securing a placement. Having Kavneet Hanspal (read Chapter 2) as a role model, especially as the first one to achieve the award in India, provided me with inspiration and a clear goal to strive towards during my CPA exams. Additionally, during the placement process, the guidance and assistance from Simandhar alumni proved invaluable in helping me prepare effectively for interviews and navigate the transition into the professional world. Their support and encouragement significantly contributed to my motivation and success throughout this journey.

Q. What advice or message would you give to someone considering Simandhar Education as their CPA exam prep institute and seeking guidance from global CPA, CMA, EA instructor, Mr. Sripal Jain?

Before delving into the reasons why I recommend Simandhar Education for your CPA journey, I want to assure you that my endorsement is completely unbiased—I'm not compensated for promoting Simandhar.

With that said, here are three key reasons why I believe Simandhar is the ideal choice:

Pre-CPA Support: The process leading up to starting your CPA journey involves numerous formalities. Simandhar's team excels in guiding you through these requirements smoothly, ensuring you can focus solely on your studies without any hassle.

Quality CPA Material: I can't stress enough the importance of using the Becker textbook for CPA studies. With its comprehensive MCQs, SIMs, and exams—both mini and full—paired with Simandhar's lectures and telegram groups, you'll have all the resources you need to excel in the CPA exam.

Post-CPA Assistance: Simandhar boasts an impressive network of tie-ups, which greatly aids alumni in securing placements swiftly. Personally, I landed a job within just three days of clearing the exam, a testament to Simandhar's strong post-CPA support system.

These factors combined make Simandhar Education the ideal choice for your CPA journey.

Q. If Simandhar Education were to organize a reality TV show, what kind of challenges or tasks would it create for the contestants to test their accounting and finance skills?

In my view, the tasks for the reality TV show could involve hands-on challenges that require a practical approach to accounting and finance concepts. For example, contestants could be tasked with calculating taxes for a hypothetical US client, ensuring compliance with relevant regulations and maximizing tax benefits. Another task could involve preparing a balance sheet using US Generally Accepted Accounting Principles (GAAP), requiring contestants to demonstrate their understanding of financial reporting standards and their ability to accurately present financial information. These tasks would not only test the contestants' technical knowledge but also their ability to apply it in real-world scenarios, making for an engaging and informative competition.

Q. What is the best part about being a Simandhar student?

Being a Simandhar student offers numerous benefits. The most significant one is the opportunity to become part of a vibrant and supportive alumni network. This network provides a valuable platform for students to connect with like-minded individuals who share similar career aspirations and goals. As a part of this community, students can access a wealth of knowledge, resources, and support that can help them navigate their academic and professional journeys more effectively. Additionally, the alumni community facilitates networking opportunities, mentorship, and collaboration, which are essential for personal and professional growth. Overall, being a Simandhar student means gaining access to a strong and supportive community that can significantly enhance one's educational experience and prospects.

Q. How much has your life changed since the day you enrolled for the course?

Since enrolling for this course, my life has undergone a remarkable transformation, charting an exciting and unprecedented path. From conquering the CPA exams to receiving prestigious awards, and now, working with a renowned Big 4 firm for over a year, every milestone has illuminated my journey with a sense of fulfillment and accomplishment. This journey has brought new challenges, opportunities, and experiences, shaping me into a more resilient and determined individual. Overall, the decision to enroll in this course has opened doors to countless possibilities and has filled my life with boundless optimism and excitement for the future.

Chapter 14

FORGING A UNIQUE PATH; FULFILLING A DREAM

Introduction:

Debdip, a B. Com graduate, embarked on the arduous path of becoming a CPA after a decade-long hiatus from his professional endeavors. Despite the break, he remained resolute in his ambition to secure a position in a prestigious Big 4 firm, even as he approached his late 40s. With the support of Simandhar Education, he was successfully placed in a KPMG audit profile, showcasing his resilience, determination, and unwavering commitment to his goals. Debdip's inspiring journey underscores the power of perseverance and reinforces the notion that age should never hinder one's pursuit of one's dreams. His story serves as a compelling testament to the idea that with dedication and perseverance, any obstacle can be overcome, and professional aspirations can be realized.

Q&A with Debdip:

Q: What inspired you to pursue a career in accounting and finance?

My decision to pursue a career in commerce was influenced by my father, a commerce graduate. In our village, prevailing opinions discouraged choosing commerce, claiming it lacked a promising future. Determined to challenge these stereotypes I aspired to excel in commerce and make him proud. I envision a day when my success will serve as a response to those doubting villagers and inspire others to choose commerce as a viable and rewarding career path.

Q. What were some of the sacrifices you had to make in your personal life while studying for the US CPA exams, and how did it feel when you finally achieved your goal?

When I began my CPA journey, I found myself juggling multiple responsibilities, including caring for my one-and-a-half year old daughter, supporting my mother, and providing for my wife. As the sole earner at home, the decision to pursue CPA was driven by the loss of my job during the COVID crisis and my struggle to secure a position in my field. This commitment required sacrificing family occasions, such as Durga Puja, a significant festival for Bengali people, as well as time with friends. The urgency to re-enter the workforce swiftly, combined with the financial constraints of potential setbacks, compelled me to maintain focus and determination.

Q. Can you share a story of someone who greatly influenced and supported you during your exam preparation, and how did their belief in you make a difference?

During my exam preparation journey, my wife played a pivotal role in supporting and motivating me. Inspired by the smiles of our daughter, she stood by me through every challenge and difficulty. Despite the financial strain and my absence due to studying, she remained steadfast in her belief in me and our dreams. Her support and reassuring words reminded me of the importance of our familial bond and encouraged me to persevere. In moments of doubt, spending time with our daughter provided me with solace and motivation. Her innocence and laughter became my source of inspiration, driving me to study diligently even during late nights while she peacefully slept. My wife's belief in me and our shared dreams made all the difference during my exam preparation journey.

Q. Can you share a funny moment that happened during your exam preparation that you still remember and laugh about?

One amusing incident that stands out from my exam preparation involves my daughter and a bit of playful banter. As the exam dates drew near, I jokingly told my daughter that I couldn't play with her because Sripal sir, my instructor, would give me punishment. To make my point, I showed her a video or photo of Sripal Sir. In response, my daughter, in her playful innocence, exclaimed, "I will beat Tipal tel!" Her adorable mispronunciation of "Sripal Sir" never fails to bring a smile to my face even now, and it served as a light-hearted moment of laughter amidst the seriousness of the exam.

Q. How has your achievement in passing the CPA exams inspired you to set higher goals and continue growing both personally and professionally?

Passing the CPA exams has instilled in me a profound sense of accomplishment and confidence. With the CPA designation under my belt, I feel equipped and empowered to take on new challenges and pursue higher goals both personally and professionally. The rigorous preparation and dedication required to achieve this milestone have honed my skills and expanded my knowledge base, making me better equipped to navigate the complexities of auditing U.S. companies and meeting the evolving demands of the professional landscape. This achievement serves as a driving force, inspiring me to continue growing and striving for excellence in all aspects of my life.

Q. How did Simandhar Education's supportive community and network of fellow students contribute to your motivation and success in passing the CPA exams and getting placed?

Simandhar Education's supportive community and network of fellow students was instrumental in my journey toward passing the CPA exams and securing a placement. The round-the-clock support provided through Telegram groups was invaluable, allowing me to quickly resolve study-related queries and stay motivated throughout the process. Engaging with experienced professionals within the community enriched my learning experience and provided valuable insights. Additionally, Simandhar's proactive placement cell played a crucial role in helping me secure a position at a prestigious Big4 firm shortly after passing the exams. The institute's strategic collaborations with various multinational companies in India and the U.S. opened up promising career opportunities for me and my fellow students. I highly recommend leveraging these resources and networks provided by Simandhar for a successful professional journey.

Q. What advice or message would you give to someone considering Simandhar Education as their CPA exam prep institute and seeking guidance from global CPA, CMA, EA instructor, Mr. Sripal Jain?

If someone is considering pursuing the CPA designation, I highly recommend Simandhar Education. Enrolling with Simandhar offers several advantages, including access to study materials from Becker Professional Education, a leading institute for CPA preparation. Additionally, students benefit from Simandhar's proprietary Learning Management System (LMS), providing valuable resources alongside Becker's materials. Live classes and the recorded lectures that were frequently updated on the platform, ensured that the latest content was available for the students. The Telegram support system is comprehensive, featuring 24/7 doubt resolution, licensing assistance, and essential placement support. My endorsement is based on personal experience (only left with licensing, which I will apply soon) rather than promotional intent. I have recommended individuals on LinkedIn, who reached out to me for CPA information, to enroll with Simandhar. The feedback received has been appreciated and they were thankful for the guidance.

Q. If Simandhar Education were to organize a reality TV show, what kind of challenges or tasks would it create for the contestants to test their accounting and finance skills?

If Simandhar Education were to organize a reality TV show, one exciting challenge could be "Deal or No Deal: Finance Edition." Contestants would negotiate finance-related deals with a twist, facing tough decisions, taking risks, and dealing with unexpected offers. The show would build anticipation as participants decide whether to accept or decline offers, testing their financial acumen, negotiation skills, and ability to handle pressure in real-life financial scenarios.

Q. What is the best part about being a Simandhar student?

The best part about being a Simandhar student is the transformative impact it has had on both my personal outlook and professional trajectory. It has not only altered how I perceive life but has also played a pivotal role in reshaping my career journey. Simandhar's comprehensive education approach has influenced my perspectives and priorities in a profound and meaningful way, equipping me with the knowledge, skills, and mindset needed to thrive in the accounting and finance industry.

Q. How much has your life changed since the day you enrolled for the course?

Since the day I enrolled in the course, my life has undergone a remarkable transformation. Initially, I harbored aspirations to contribute my skills to multinational corporations. However, despite my 12-year tenure in the Indian unorganized sector, transitioning to the corporate realm posed significant challenges. Yet, upon enrolling in the CPA program, I witnessed a profound shift. Doors to opportunities began to open, culminating in my successful placement within one of the Big4 firms. Now, I find myself contemplating the prospect of a US rotation, a testament to the transformative power of this experience. This journey has not only altered my future outlook but has also instilled in me a sense of optimism about the myriad opportunities unfolding on my professional path. Indeed, attaining the status of a qualified CPA has been instrumental in facilitating this remarkable achievement.

A LEGACY OF TRANSFORMATION

As I reflect on the journey of Simandhar Education and my role as its co-founder, I am filled with a profound sense of accomplishment and gratitude. What began as a vision to uplift the student community and provide them with robust professional training has now blossomed into a transformative educational powerhouse. The story of Simandhar Education is not just one of success but one of perseverance, innovation, and a relentless pursuit of excellence.

The Evolution of Simandhar Education

Simandhar Education started with a simple yet powerful mission: to bridge the gap between Indian professionals and global opportunities. Recognizing the immense potential and talent in our country, we sought to provide world-class training in CPA (Certified Public Accountant) and CMA (Certified Management Accountant) certifications, which are gateways to prestigious careers worldwide. Our partnership with Becker and CPA Practice Advisor is a testament to our commitment to quality education, ensuring our students receive the best possible resources and training.

From our humble beginnings, we have expanded our course offerings to include EA (Enrolled Agent), CIA (Certified Internal Auditor), and IFRS (International Financial Reporting Standards) certifications. This diversification has allowed us to cater to a broader spectrum of students and professionals, each with unique aspirations and career goals. Our growth is reflected in the success of our students, who now occupy esteemed positions in multinational corporations, contributing to the global economy with their skills and expertise.

Key Milestones and Achievements

One of the defining moments in our journey was receiving the Best Edupreneur Award from the Government of Telangana in 2018. This accolade was not just a recognition of our hard work but also an affirmation of our impact on the education sector. It reinforced our belief that education is not merely about imparting knowledge but about transforming lives.

Our collaborations with industry giants such as Ernst and Young, Deloitte, Invesco, and Virtusa Polaris have been instrumental in shaping our curriculum and training methodologies. These partnerships have enabled us to provide tailored corporate training sessions, ensuring that our students are not only academically proficient but also industry-ready. Companies like Wells Fargo, D. E. Shaw, AIG, Microsoft, Synchrony, Amazon, Infosys, Reliance Jio, and Reliance Industries have trusted us to upskill their workforce, a responsibility we take with utmost seriousness.

Transforming Education: Vision and Mission

At Simandhar Education, our vision is to upskill professionals and students by fostering a culture of continuous learning. We believe that in a rapidly changing world, adaptability and lifelong learning are key to success. Our mission is to provide a standard of learning that can truly transform lives, equipping our students with the knowledge and skills necessary to excel in their careers.

Our purpose is rooted in the belief that education goes beyond the mere dissemination of information. It is about transformation—transforming students into well-rounded professionals who can navigate the complexities of the global economy with confidence and competence. This philosophy is encapsulated in one of my favorite quotes: "Education is not just information; it's transformation."

Personal Journey and Reflections

Being a first-generation entrepreneur, co-founder, and lead instructor of Simandhar Education LLP (CPA Practice Advisor's channel partner in India), I am an innovative and skilled professional with over a decade of industry experience in Audit, Corporate Finance, IFRS, GAAP, ICFR (SOX-404), and Finance. I am also one of LinkedIn top US accounting industry's influencers with more than 60K followers. Industry Era named me one of the "10 Best Education Leaders of 2021," and the Progressive Academy awarded me the title of "Best Edupreneur of Telangana (India) 2018."

Looking back at my personal journey, I am reminded of the words of Steve Jobs: "I'm convinced that about half of what separates successful entrepreneurs from the non-successful ones is pure perseverance." These words have resonated with me throughout my career, guiding me through challenges and inspiring me to keep pushing forward.

My career path was conventional, working with renowned multinational companies. However, I felt a deeper calling to contribute to the student community. Teaching part-time at a CA institute revealed the struggles and aspirations of many students, and I realized there was a significant gap in the support system for those pursuing professional certifications. This realization was the spark that ignited the creation of Simandhar Education.

Passion and Quality Teaching

"Passion and quality teaching made me successful. To become a good entrepreneur, always trust yourself and work towards your goals." This belief has been the cornerstone of my approach to education and entrepreneurship. At Simandhar Education, we prioritize passion and quality in everything we do. Our faculty comprises industry experts and seasoned professionals who bring real-world experience into the classroom, enriching the learning experience for our students.

Our commitment to quality is reflected in our rigorous curriculum, comprehensive study materials, and personalized mentorship programs. We understand that each student is unique, and we strive to provide tailored support to help them achieve their individual goals. Whether it's through one-on-one tutoring, career counseling, or interactive workshops, we are dedicated to our students' success.

Future Prospects and Continuing the Legacy

As we look to the future, the prospects for Simandhar Education are incredibly promising. The demand for professional certifications continues to grow, and we are poised to meet this demand with innovative programs and cutting-edge training methodologies. Our focus will remain on expanding our course offerings, forging new industry partnerships, and leveraging technology to enhance the learning experience.

One of our key future initiatives is to develop an online learning platform that provides flexible, accessible, and high-quality education to students worldwide. This platform will incorporate interactive modules, virtual classrooms, and AI-driven personalized learning paths, ensuring that our students receive the best possible education regardless of their location.

Additionally, we plan to expand our corporate training programs, offering customized solutions to companies seeking to upskill their workforce in areas such as finance, accounting, and management. By staying attuned to industry trends and emerging technologies, we aim to provide training that is relevant, practical, and impactful.

The Role of Community and Feedback

The success of Simandhar Education is a testament to the strength of our community. Our students, alumni, faculty, and partners have all played a crucial role in shaping our journey. We value their feedback and insights, which help us continually improve and evolve. Engaging with our community through regular surveys, focus groups, and feedback sessions allows us to understand their needs better and respond effectively.

Our alumni network is a source of immense pride and inspiration. Seeing our former students achieve remarkable success in their careers reaffirms our mission and motivates us to keep pushing the boundaries of education. We are committed to maintaining strong connections with our alumni, providing them with ongoing support and opportunities for professional development.

The Human Touch: Empathy and Understanding

Despite the advances in technology and the increasing emphasis on digital learning, we believe that the human touch remains essential in education. Empathy, understanding, and personalized attention are at the heart of our approach. We recognize that each student faces unique challenges and aspirations, and we strive to create an environment where they feel supported and empowered.

Our faculty and staff are trained to provide not only academic guidance but also emotional support, helping students navigate the pressures and stresses of their educational journey. We believe that a holistic approach to education, one that addresses the mind, body, and spirit, is key to fostering true transformation.

Final Thoughts

As I conclude this reflection on the journey of Simandhar Education and my role within it, I am filled with a deep sense of pride and fulfilment. Our story is one of passion, perseverance, and a relentless pursuit of excellence. We have transformed the lives of countless students, equipping them with the knowledge and skills to excel on the global stage.

However, our journey is far from over. The world of education is constantly evolving, and we are committed to staying at the forefront of this transformation. With a steadfast belief in the power of education and a deep commitment to our students, we will continue to innovate, inspire, and impact lives.

To all our students, past, present, and future: thank you for being a part of our journey. Your success is our greatest reward, and we are honored to be a part of your story. Together we will continue to strive for excellence, break new ground, and make a lasting difference in the world.

In the words of Steve Jobs, "The people who are crazy enough to think they can change the world are the ones who do." At Simandhar Education, we believe in the power of dreams, the strength of perseverance, and the transformative potential of education. Let us continue to dream big, work hard, and change the world—one student at a time.

MORE ABOUT OUR SUCCESS STORIES

Vaishnavi Patel (Chapter 7) is now with American Express.

Bobby Agrawal (Chapter 8) has since been promoted to VP at Standard Chartered Bank.

Surya Teja (Chapter 9) is now permanently settled in the US with a H1 B visa.

ABOUT THE AUTHOR

Sripal Jain is a highly accomplished professional with a strong commitment to education. He's a qualified Chartered Accountant (CA) and Certified Public Accountant (CPA), leveraging his expertise to co-found Simandhar Education, a remote learning institute focused on CPA, CMA and other professional courses' training.

Sripal's influence extends far beyond the classroom. Recognized as a leader in the accounting and finance field, he's a sought-after speaker. From industry giants like Microsoft and Reliance to international conferences like AICPA Engage, he shares his knowledge and insights with a global audience.

Driven by a passion for education, Sripal believes it has the power to transform lives. This conviction is central to his approach at Simandhar Education. The focus is on delivering the highest standards of learning, empowering students and professionals to achieve their full potential. His dedication extends beyond academics; Sripal is a strong advocate for lifelong learning and student success, fostering a student-centric environment that sets high expectations and supports career aspirations.

Connect with the Author

LinkedIn: Sripal Jain (CA, CPA)

Instagram: sripal.ca.uscpa

FaceBook: Sripal Jain

Email: sripaljain07@gmail.com

www.ingramcontent.com/pod-product-compliance
Lightning Source LLC
LaVergne TN
LVHW021144160826
845679LV00023B/2034
* 9 7 9 8 8 9 4 9 8 3 5 2 3 *